# THE EARTH STRIKES BACK

## HOW WE USE AND ABUSE OUR PLANET

# WILDLIFE

Arthur Haswell

**Thameside Press**

Distributed in the United States by
Smart Apple Media
1980 Lookout Drive
North Mankato, MN56003

Copyright © Belitha Press Limited 2000
Text copyright © Arthur Haswell 2000

**Series Editor** Mary-Jane Wilkins
**Editor** Molly Perham
**Designer** Helen James
**Picture researcher** Kathy Lockley
**Illustrator** William Donohoe
**Consultant** Chris Baines

Printed in China

9  8  7  6  5  4  3  2  1

**Library of Congress Cataloging-in-Publication Data**
Haswell, Arthur.
  Wildlife / by Arthur Haswell.
    p.cm.—(Earth strikes back)
  Includes index.
  Summary: Examines major environmental issues
surrounding wildlife, giving examples of attempts
to solve global problems and sources for more
information.
  ISBN 1-929298-61-7
  1. Natural history—Juvenile literature. 2.
Ecology—Juvenile literature. [1. Natural history.
2. Ecology.] I. Title. II. Series.

  QH48.H37 2000
  333.95—dc21
                                    00-022290

**Photographic credits:**
Britstock-Ifa / Andre Gerard 30, /Diaf
/J D Sudres 11 T
Bruce Coleman /Norbert Schwirtz 21 T, /Staffan
Widstrand 28 B
Ecoscene /Gryniewicz 45, /Harwood 44
Hutchison Library /Leslie Smith 7 B, /Nigel Smith 20,
/Robert Franics 11 B, /W. Jesco von Puttkamer 5
NHPA /ANT 31 T, /Daryl Balfour 14, /G I Bernard 8,
13, /Laurie Campbell 37 T, /G J Cambridge 33 R,
/Michael Leach 35 L, /Mike Lane 16 T, /Nobert Wu 8,
/Stephen Dalton 37 B, /T Kitchen & V Hurst 12 B
Panos Pictures /Eric Miller 23 B
Science Photo Library /Dr Jeremy Burgess 31 B,
/John Reader 8, /Mehau Kulyk 12 T
Frank Spooner Pictures 27, 28 T
Still Pictures /Arnold Newman 24 B,
/Compost/Visage 40 B, /Dave Watts 26, /EIA 22
/Francois Gilson/Bios 7 T, /Fred Bavendam 25, /Fritz
Polking 4, 16 B, /Georges Lopez/Bios 32, /J P
Delobelle 19 B, /John Caucalosi 17 B, /Kevin Schafer
18, 24 T, /Klein/Hubert 17 T, 36 T, /Leonard Lessin 35
R, /Mark Carwadine 40 T, /Michel Gunther 6, 34,
/Noel Matoff 29, /Olivier Legrand 19 T, /Roland Seitre
41, /S C Denis-Huet 21 B, /Thomas D Mangelsen 15 B,
/Yves Thouerieus 15 T
Sygma/Robert King 23 T
World Wildlife Fund Photo Library/Olivier
Langrand 33 L

Words in **bold** are explained in the glossary
on pages 46 and 47.

# Contents

# A living world

*We share our world with more than a million different wild animals and 350,000 different kinds of plant. The range of species is enormous, and new animals and plants are still being discovered.*

▲ *The natural habitat of the giant panda is the bamboo forests high in the mountains of southwestern China and eastern Tibet.*

## Birth, life, and death

Every part of the world has its own mix of **wildlife**. Climate and landscape vary from place to place, and this produces different sets of living conditions, or **habitats**. Animals and plants have different characteristics that help them to live in a particular habitat, but their lives all follow a similar pattern.

## Humans and animals

Until humans appeared, all life on Earth was wild. For many thousands of years, humans lived in balance with nature. Early humans hunted wild animals to eat and for their skins, and people also gathered food and wood from wild plants.

◄ *On this lakeside, some plants live in the water, some on the shore, while others prefer higher ground. Fish, rabbits, birds, and butterflies also live in different parts of the biosphere.*

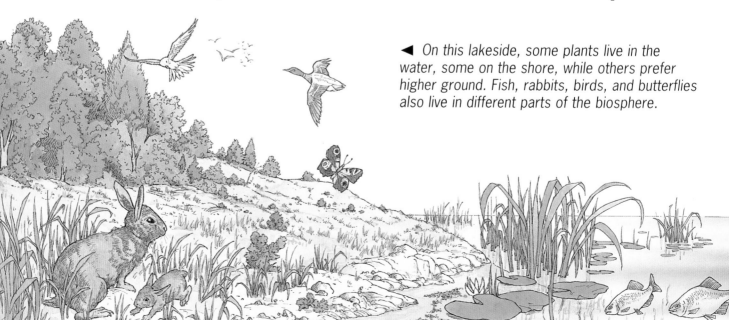

▲ *A hunting party of Urueu-Wau-Wau Indians in Brazil sets out to kill and bring home animals to eat.*

## Hunter-gatherers

Today, some tribal people still live in groups as **hunter-gatherers**. They live in large areas of natural land, with a wide range of wildlife around them. They usually hunt only when they are hungry and rarely kill more than they need. In this way tribes of hunter-gatherers ensure that there will be enough food in the future.

## The spread of life

All life exists within the **biosphere**, the layer around our planet between the upper atmosphere and the ocean floor. Plants and animals that share the same habitat may live in different parts of it, each choosing the place that suits them best. For example, three similar birds feed in coniferous trees in North America. The cape may warbler feeds at the top of the trees, the bay-breasted warbler chooses the middle, while the myrtle warbler stays on the lower branches.

## Making peace with our planet

Throughout history, wildlife has suffered at the hands of humans. From stone axe, through bow and arrow, to the latest gun and nuclear warhead, we have gained greater and greater power over the life around us. The pollution that we produce kills wildlife, and as we destroy the natural places where wild animals and plants live, we wipe out many **species**. In the past, the slow rate of **extinction** has been matched by the **evolution** of new species. But now, the rate at which wild plants and animals are being wiped out is increasing. The number of species is falling, and no one knows how this will affect the Earth or us. We need to make peace with our planet, and allow the wildlife of today to survive into the future.

In this way, each bird has its own particular part of the forest to itself. Wildlife coexists in a similar way throughout the biosphere, in each different habitat.

# Wildlife and us

*Humans are the most successful and adaptable animals. In the past, our success has been at the expense of other animals and plants. But now, we use our skills to protect wildlife.*

▲ *In Ethiopia, wolves have been wrongly blamed for killing sheep as farms have spread.*

## The first farmers

When early hunter-gatherers started to keep animals and grow crops, their relationship with the wildlife around them changed. Farming started about 11,000 years ago around the eastern end of the Mediterranean in present-day Turkey, Syria, Lebanon, and Israel. People sowed wild wheat and barley, and kept sheep, pigs, cows and goats. Gradually throughout Europe, Asia, and the Americas people turned to farming. For the first time, land was cleared of its natural covering of trees and bushes to make way for crops and livestock. The areas left for wildlife began to shrink.

## Wiping out wolves

In Britain, before farming began, the wolf population was about 7,000. There were about 14,000 bears and about 6,000 lynx. The spread of farming had a devastating effect on these animals, because now they were regarded as **predators** that might attack farm animals. Folk tales such as *Little Red Riding Hood* and *The Three Little Pigs* show wolves as clever and wicked—but in fact most hardly bother people. Britain's wild bears and wolves were killed long ago, and although there are still a few brown bears left in Europe, their numbers are small.

## Return of the bears

The situation is similar throughout the world. In Africa, for example, there are fewer than 1,000 Ethiopian wolves left. But now, it seems that attitudes may be changing. Bears have been released recently in the European Alps. Some French farmers protested, but Austrian farmers have found the bears to be harmless—and are helping to ensure their survival.

▲ *Released into the wild, this brown bear lives as its ancestors did in the French Alps.*

## Endangered species

A species with a small population living in protected areas is called **rare**. Species that are plentiful in some places, but are reducing in numbers worldwide, are described as **threatened**. When a species seems likely to become **extinct**, we call it **endangered**. Looking after the natural environment for the benefit of wildlife is called **conservation**.

In recent years, people have become more committed to conservation. Throughout most of the world, laws have been passed that make it illegal to kill endangered animals or pick. endangered plants. There are now more than 1,200 national parks and reserves worldwide where rare species

Wildlife is important in many ways. Every plant and animal adds to the beauty of nature—and, because each is dependent on others, every species plays a part in the survival of life on Earth. From the human point of view, the study of wildlife teaches us about ourselves and the world around us. For example, studying wildlife has helped scientists discover medicines to treat human illnesses.

are protected—but the world's wildlife is still under pressure. Growing populations mean more mouths to feed and so farmers clear more land for growing crops. Use of **herbicides** and **pesticides** can poison wildlife. The battle between conservation and destruction is likely to continue.

▲ *Rangers protect wildlife and show tourists around the Sharmwari Reserve in South Africa.*

# The story of life

*Life has flourished on Earth for millions of years. During that time many different plant and animal species developed. Some became extinct long ago, but others have survived.*

## First life

Tiny **bacteria** that were fossilized in rock nearly four billion years ago are the earliest form of life found so far. Each one consists of a single cell, the smallest living thing that can exist. (The human body, by contrast, is made up of billions of cells.) Over a period of a billion years, a new type of bacteria, **cyanobacteria**, evolved. These could take energy from the Sun, as modern plants do, and were the basis of all the plant life found on Earth today.

▼ *This diagram shows the succession of life, from simple species on the seabed, to plants that conquered land, the animals that followed, and human beings.*

▲ *Cyanobacteria often grouped together to form dense structures. This mass of preserved cyanobacteria in Australia is 2–3 billion years old.*

## Evolution

Like modern plants, cyanobacteria gave out the gas **oxygen**, which began to build up in the sea and air. New species of bacteria evolved that used the oxygen as a fuel to burn food, like our own bodies. From these **aerobic** bacteria, all the animals that we know today have evolved. Sea creatures with soft bodies, such as jellyfish and sponges, were the first to evolve.

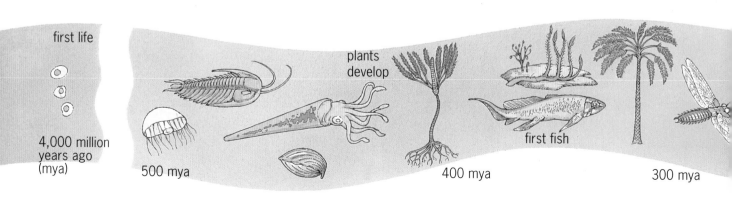

first life

4,000 million years ago (mya)

500 mya

plants develop

first fish

400 mya

300 mya

## Trilobites

About 600 million years ago, animals with hard skeletons evolved. There were hundreds of different species of **trilobites**, many burrowing into the mud on the sea floor. Rock that was formed at that time contains their fossilized bodies, ranging in size from ¼ inch to more than 26 inches. Trilobites existed until about 200 million years ago, when they became extinct. By then, the ancestors of today's marine wildlife were evolving. Fish and sharks swam in the sea. Reptiles came out of the water to live on land for the first time, and from them mammals evolved.

## Clues to the past

**Fossils** are a clue to the type of plants and animals that lived long ago. The discovery of huge fossilized bones led to our knowledge of the dinosaurs. Fossils from more recent times preserve the remains of animals similar to those of today. In Baluchistan, in southwest Asia, the remains of a huge rhinoceros 13 feet high have been found, while the woolly rhinoceros and the woolly mammoth roamed the colder parts of North America, Europe, and Asia.

## Living fossils

At about the same time that creatures came out of the sea to live on the land, strange fish swam in the oceans. Fossils of coelacanths from up to 350 million years ago show a creature 5 feet long, with pairs of jointed fins like feet and hands. Scientists assumed that the coelacanths became extinct 65 million years ago, but then a living specimen (below) was caught in the Indian Ocean in 1938. Since then, more than 200 have been found around the Comoros Islands. The local fisherman had regularly caught about ten coelacanths each year. In 1989, the Comoros Islanders' canoes were replaced with motor boats and the fishermen began catching four times as many fish. More than 60 percent of the coelacanths counted in that year had gone by 1994.

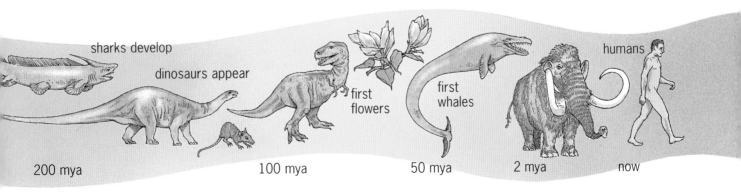

sharks develop

dinosaurs appear

first flowers

first whales

humans

200 mya          100 mya          50 mya          2 mya          now

# Grouping wildlife

*Scientists sort animals and plants into different groups. As our knowledge has increased, those groupings have changed and become more complicated.*

## Harmful or useful?

For early humans, wildlife was either harmful or useful. Snakes, big cats, and poisonous plants were harmful. Animals that provided meat were useful. Cave paintings in France, dating from 18,000 years ago, show useful animals such as deer, bison, mammoths, and woolly rhinoceroses. All these were hunted for food.

◄ *Animals with similar bodies or ways of surviving in the wild are grouped together in classes.*

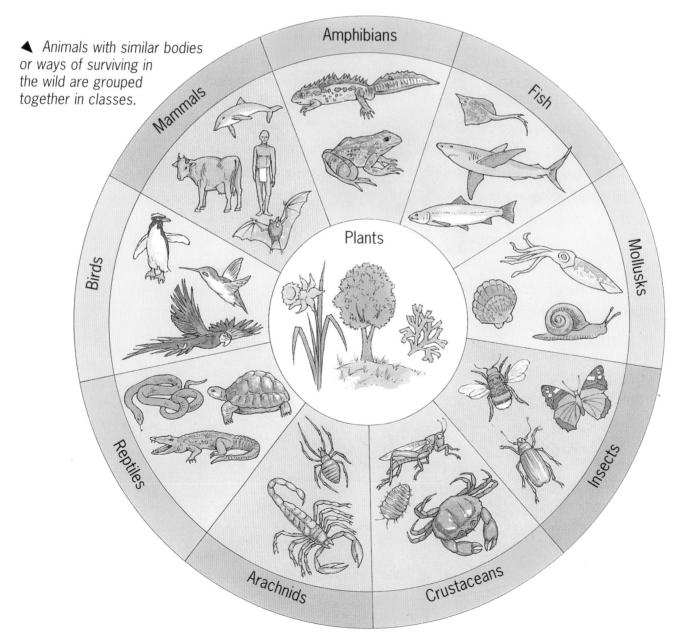

▲ *Cave paintings at Lascaux, France, show the animals that were important to prehistoric people 18,000 years ago.*

## Aristotle's ideas

More than 2,000 years ago, the Greek philosopher Aristotle wrote down his ideas about wildlife. At that time, only about 1,000 species were known. Aristotle put all the animals with red blood and a backbone in one group or class, and those without red blood or a backbone in the other. Plants were classified as trees, shrubs, or herbs. Aristotle was able to fit all the known species of his time into this system, which remained in use for the next 2,000 years.

## Two-part names

By the time Carl Linnaeus, a Swedish naturalist, began studying wildlife in the 1720s, thousands more species had been discovered. He developed a new way of classifying animals and plants by grouping together species that were similar. All animals that looked like cats were called *Felis*, the Latin word for cat. Each species was then described with a second Latin word. So every animal and plant was given two Latin words. This became

Modern classification is based on a number of systems. Bacteria are best described by **phenetic classification**, which sees them as a large group of tiny creatures working together. **Orthodox classification** looks at shared features in plants and animals. In **cladistics**, only features shared by all members of a group are taken into account. These systems of classification are helped by the latest studies of **DNA**, the chemical mix that sets each species apart.

their **scientific name**. Everywhere in the world people use Linnaeus' two-part name to ensure they are talking about the same plant or animal.

Linnaeus did not stop there, going on to divide all living things into the two kingdoms of plants and animals. These kingdoms were each divided again and again—seven times in all.

▼ *These are the young of the species* Homo sapiens. *In Latin* Homo *means "human" and* sapiens *means "wise."*

# Extinction

*When the last animal or plant of a species dies, that species is extinct. Since life began on Earth, millions of species have developed and become extinct.*

▲ *These bones fossilized in rock belong to a Gasosaurus, a dinosaur that lived about 150 million years ago.*

## The end of the dinosaurs

Dinosaurs dominated the Earth for 140 million years. These reptiles lived both on the land and in the sea. Then, 65 million years ago, all dinosaur species became extinct. No one can be certain why this happened. Some scientists think a huge amount of dust entered the atmosphere, blocking the Sun. Plants could not grow properly, so plant-eating dinosaurs starved and flesh-eaters, in turn, had no food. The dust-cloud, which stayed in the air for years, may have been caused by a volcanic eruption. Other scientists think that a meteor crashed into the Earth. Whatever happened, the effect was devastating, causing the biggest mass extinction the world has seen.

## Human hunters

In prehistoric times, as humans spread out across the land, more and more animals became **prey**. Species that we no longer find on Earth were hunted by humans, who had developed the skill of making stone axes. Woolly mammoths and woolly rhinoceroses lived on the Great Plains of North America, in Europe and in India. Then, about 10,000 years ago, they disappeared— probably hunted to extinction.

Humans have continued to wipe out plant and animal species, and in recent years this has been happening faster than ever before. Two or three species become extinct naturally each year, but now the figure is more than a thousand. Some scientists predict that in the twenty-first century, humans will cause the extinction of 66 percent of all bird, mammal, butterfly, and plant species. This would be the greatest mass extinction since the dinosaurs died.

## Natural cures

Each species carries a unique set of **genes** that determine its character and chemical mix. When a species becomes extinct, those unique genes disappear. About 25 percent of modern medicines use chemical compounds first discovered in plants.

◀ *These American bison live safely in Yellowstone National Park, but 100 years ago the species faced extinction.*

In the nineteenth century, European settlers reduced the herds of 20 million bison that grazed the Great Plains of the U.S. to 551 animals. Laws were passed banning hunting, and now 30,000 bison live safely in U.S. and Canadian parks. An even more extraordinary revival may be performed by the quagga (below). This cousin of the zebra became extinct when the last one died at Amsterdam Zoo in 1883. It was stuffed and taken to the museum, where it is still on display. **Zoologists** tested the stuffed quagga and found that, underneath its skin, it was the same as modern zebras. Now they are trying to revive the species by selecting zebras that look like quaggas and breeding them.

But the number of plant species is becoming smaller as natural habitats are destroyed. No one knows if genes that could have cured future diseases have been lost forever.

# Living together

*Plants and animals depend on their neighbors. In any area, the wildlife relies on other species for food and survival.*

## Food for all

Plants provide food for many animals. **Grazing animals**, such as voles and zebra, take **nutrients** from plants into their bodies. They are themselves the food of meat-eaters, such as cats and lions. The meat-eaters take nutrients from plant-eating animals. The movement of nutrients from plant to vole to cat, or from plant to zebra to lion, is called a **food chain**.

At the top of many food chains are humans. For example, humans eat beef that comes from cows that graze on grass.

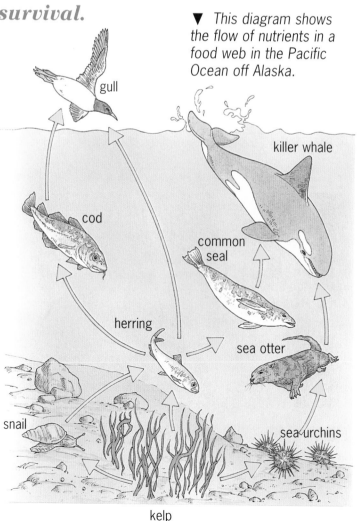

▼ *This diagram shows the flow of nutrients in a food web in the Pacific Ocean off Alaska.*

gull

killer whale

cod

common seal

herring

sea otter

snail

sea urchins

kelp

◄ *A lioness preys on plant-eating animals such as zebra and antelope. She is at the top of the food chain.*

## Caught in the web

In any **bio-region**, different animals have a variety of food. The food chains are joined in **food webs**. A natural balance ensures that there are enough plants or animals in each species to feed those above in the chain. If the population of one species falls, the whole food web can suffer.

## Trouble at sea

There are fewer fish off Alaska these days. Fishing boats have taken huge catches and climate change has warmed the ocean, driving many of the remaining fish north to cooler water. The loss of so many fish has affected a whole food web. Fish-eating birds have starved, and so have seals and sea-lions. Killer whales, which used to feed on seals and sea lions, have begun eating sea otters.

Food webs can be disrupted by warmer water, and this is not always caused by humans. Every five or six years, the winds that normally blow east to west across the Pacific Ocean die down. Warm water from Indonesia drifts towards America. No one knows the reason for this, but **El Niño**, as it is called, causes floods, disease, and ruined crops as far away as Africa. The warm water reduces the amount of seaweed and krill. The number of fish falls and seals and sea-lions (right) starve. During El Niño in 1997, 75 percent of baby sea lions along the U.S. coast died.

▲ *This sea otter is resting on a rock covered with kelp. The species is suffering from overfishing.*

The sea otter's favourite food is sea urchins. With fewer sea otters to eat them, sea urchins have prospered.

Kelp is a type of seaweed, with fronds up to 215 feet long, that grows in forests on the ocean floor. Many marine animals live on kelp, including sea urchins. With so many sea urchins, the kelp forests are shrinking. Fish are starving, leaving even less for seals and sea lions to eat. These changes in the north-eastern Pacific Ocean will continue until a new balance is established.

# Wetlands

*Wetlands are areas where seas, lakes, and rivers touch land. Some wetlands stretch hundreds of miles along coasts; others surround small ponds. All are rich in wildlife, but they are easily destroyed.*

▲ *The Iberian lynx is just over 3 feet long. It hunts at night for rabbits and other small mammals.*

## When the dam burst

In Spain, the River Guadiamar broadens over a vast, low plain before entering the Atlantic Ocean. Migrating birds stop there, and it is the home of the world's most endangered cat, the Iberian lynx. Much of the wetland is protected as a nature reserve, the Coto Doñana.

In April, 1998, a dam holding back poisonous waste from a mine collapsed. The river turned red and little was done to stop the flow of poison down to Doñana. Over 12,000 acres were affected and thousands of birds and fish died. A year later, half the over-wintering geese were found to be poisoned, and storks, cormorants, and herons are thought to be at risk. No one can predict the long-term effects on wildlife of Spain's worst ecological disaster.

## The Pantanal

The world's largest wetland lies in the middle of South America. Based around the River Paraguay, the Pantanal is a vast area of flooded grassland and forests. Millions of fish provide food for a wide range of birds and animals, including endangered species such as caiman alligators, hyacinth macaws, and blue macaws.

► *Already threatened by poachers, the caiman alligator could become extinct as the Pantanal changes.*

▲ *The hyacinth macaw's habitat spreads into four countries, making it difficult to protect.*

A giant canal, 2,100 kilometres long, is being built to allow ships into the heart of the country. The canal will alter the flow of water across the Pantanal. The wetlands can absorb heavy rainfall by spreading the extra water over a wide area, but the canal will channel all the water downstream and may cause floods. Wetland plants are sensitive to even small changes in water level, and could be devastated. Only one percent of the area is protected by law. Environmentalists are working with the builders of the canal to help protect the wildlife.

The Everglades in southern Florida covers 3,100 square miles. Rainfall is high, and this vast area of low, flat land lies under shallow water. Because the water moves slowly through saw-grass, the Everglades is nicknamed The River of Grass. The area is home to a wide range of wildlife, including the endangered Florida panther (below). Large parts of the Everglades have been drained and turned into farmland. Chemical run-off from fertilizers and pesticides has polluted the water. Towns have been built, and drinking water has to be provided for six million people. Now an expensive clean-up is under way, which will be the largest U.S. public works project ever. The water flow will be restored, pollution cleared, and the wildlife will be saved.

# Forests

*All over the world, different types of forest have survived for thousands of years. Natural forests provide homes for a rich concentration of wildlife.*

### Rain forest

Warmth and moisture make rain forests the richest **eco-systems** on Earth. They have existed for thousands of years, with young plants and animals replacing the old, and each species dependent on others. But the range of lumber attracts loggers, who cut the trees and clear the land. Trees such as mahogany and ebony are endangered because so many have been logged.

▲ *The quetzal, one of the most beautiful birds in the world, is endangered.*

## Timber!

Lumber is big business. Each year wood products from the millions of trees that are cut worldwide are worth over $105 billion. But wood processing is wasteful, because more than 50 percent of the wood taken into a sawmill is thrown away as dust or chips. Even some wood is wasted In the U.S., about 20 percent of processed wood is made into packing cases, which are used once and then discarded. In future, new techniques and recycling will make better use of trees that are cut.

In the Central American rain forests, the quetzal (sometimes called the most beautiful bird on Earth) feeds on fruit, including wild avocados. The logging industry has cut down many of the fruit-bearing trees. Now quetzals are an endangered species.

### Dry forests

In places where hot forests receive little rain, a different kind of eco-system has evolved. In the dry forests of Madagascar, there are many plants and animals found

▲ *The Madagascan greater mouse lemur joined the list of endangered species as soon as it was discovered there are so few of them.*

nowhere else in the world, including the plowshare tortoise and the recently discovered mouse lemur. Perhaps the strangest animal is the giant jumping rat, which has long ears and moves like a rabbit. It exists only in a 16 square mile area of dry forest. Although Madagascar has begun to look after its rain forests, the dry forests are mostly unprotected. Their rich range of wildlife is under threat as loggers and farmers clear the trees.

## Temperate forest

About 7,000 years ago, forests of mixed broadleaf and coniferous trees covered much of Europe and the eastern U.S. Plants of all sizes supported a range of animals. The forests have gradually been cleared, and only one percent of the European temperate forest remains, mostly in Finland and Sweden. In the U.S., the temperate forests that remain have nearly all been logged. Some have been replaced with plantations containing only a single species of evergreen tree. Most wildlife cannot make a home there.

▼ *In this plantation, Norway spruce is the only species of tree. The trees grow straight and fast, but do not create a good habitat for wildlife.*

# Grasslands

*Grassland covers about 25 percent of the world's land and produces 90 percent of our food. Wildlife has mostly been replaced by crops, or by herds of cows, sheep, or goats.*

## Hot grasslands

Grassland in tropical countries is called **savannah**. The savannah of Brazil lies south of the great rain forest. This area, the Campo Cerrado, is dry for most of the year and yellow grass covers the land.

▲ *In the wet season, water floods the Brazilian savannah, bringing islands of fresh, green growth.*

Then, in summer, thunderstorms drench the soil and the Campo Cerrado turns green. A unique range of plants grows among the grass, including orchids and shrubs related to pineapples. Animals have to survive in a harsh environment, yet many insects and rodents thrive.

Surface mines have stripped the land on the Campo Cerrado and crops such as sugar beet and soybeans have been sown in the thin soil. Its unique wildlife has suffered as a result.

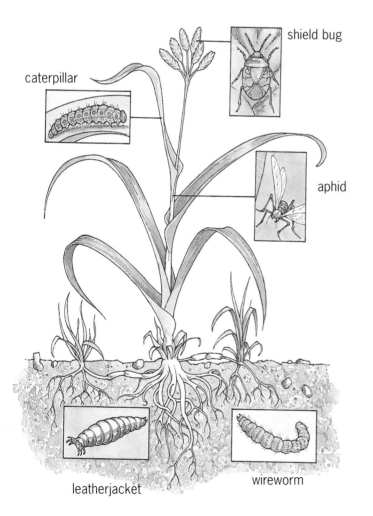

caterpillar

shield bug

aphid

leatherjacket

wireworm

◄ *A single grass plant supports a variety of wildlife, both above the ground and beneath the soil.*

## Bring on the elephants

Studies of Kenya's Tsavo National Park have shown that the savannah needs elephants just as much as the elephants need the savannah. Elephant herds strip the leaves from trees and bushes, encouraging new growth (below). Any seeds that are swallowed are softened in the elephants' guts. Later, far away, the seeds are left on the ground in dung, which provides the perfect fertilizer for new plants.

▲ *The beautiful sawfly orchid cannot be cultivated, and large quantities of plants are taken from the wild.*

## Cool grasslands

The cool grasslands that have survived cover some of the loneliest places on Earth. The Eurasian steppes, which stretch from Turkey almost to the Pacific coast of China, are vast open spaces where grass and wild flowers such as orchids thrive. Grazing animals and rodents eat the plants. Shrews, foxes, and snakes eat other animals.

Orchids are prized for their beauty, and many have been dug up to be sold to gardeners around the world. In Turkey, about 20 million orchids were dug up from the grasslands every year. But now village nurseries have been set up to produce corms, tubers, and bulbs for export—rather than digging up wild flowers.

# Poachers and traders

*Many species are threatened by the demands of people who value them only as a source of medicine, or as a luxury food. These people encourage illegal poaching and trade.*

## Tiger bones

In traditional Chinese medicine, ground tiger bones are used to treat many illnesses, ranging from skin diseases to laziness. People are willing to pay a lot of money for tiger-bone medicines. Though the tiger is a protected species in India, **poachers** are willing to break the law because of the rich rewards. A dead tiger is worth over $50 000.

The U.S. is still a large market for illegal wildlife products. Traditional medicines containing tiger bones are openly on sale in New York. One wild tiger is illegally killed everyday, and with only 5,000 left, the tiger may become extinct in the wild within ten years— unless the illegal trade is stopped.

▼ *This medicine store in Taiwan is stocked with tiger heads, shark fins, and other parts of endangered animals.*

▲ *These Russian poachers have killed and opened a sturgeon to remove its eggs.*

## Sturgeon wars

The eggs of the sturgeon fish, sold in shops as caviar, fetch about $750 per pound. More than 90 percent of the world's caviar comes from sturgeon in the Caspian Sea. Until recently, strict laws stopped too many sturgeon being caught—but gangs armed with machine guns have taken control. Today, 85 percent of the caviar sold in Russia has been taken illegally. If the gangs are not stopped within the next two years, there may be no sturgeon left in the Caspian Sea.

## Barbecued eels

European eels are great travelers. The **larvae** are born in the Sargasso Sea, in the Caribbean. They develop into tiny transparent glass eels and swim 3,700 miles to Europe, where they live in the rivers and turn into elvers before returning to the Sargasso. Eels are a source of food for other wild animals, and in particular otters and birds.

Billions of glass eels make another journey, never reaching adulthood. The Japanese like to barbecue them. About three million tiny glass eels make up one ton—and the Japanese eat 55,000 tons every year. There are no laws to stop the trade, which is endangering European eels and the wildlife that feeds on them.

## Community guards

Rhinoceros horn has been used as a medicine in China for more than 4,000 years. To protect the remaining rhinos, the trade has been made illegal. But poachers are able to sell the horns for high prices, and they are still killing the rhinos. In Namibia, Southwest Africa, local people have been trained to become guards. Using their knowledge of wildlife, they patrol areas around their homes and remove horns from rhinos to stop them being killed (below). Poaching has decreased, but Namibia earns money from tourists who come to see the rhinos.

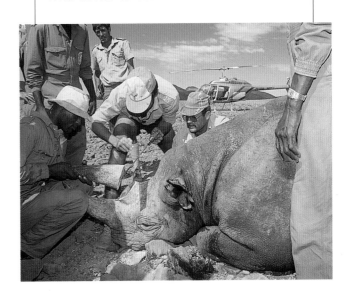

# Climate change

*Climates around the world are changing as the pollution that we have pumped into the air warms the atmosphere. Even the smallest change in climate affects wildlife.*

## The Siberian tiger

The few remaining Siberian tigers —about 400 of them—live in forests on remote Russian mountains. Every year, as the climate changes, their home gets warmer and wetter. By the year 2010, the average temperature of their habitat may have increased by 3°F, which would make it suitable for farming. In the future, the forests could be cleared to make way for fields, and then the Siberian tiger would have nowhere to live.

▲ *This Siberian tiger lies peacefully in the snow—but how much longer can it survive?*

## Water testers

Reptiles are particularly sensitive to changes in climate and environment. In Costa Rica, the golden toad has recently become extinct because its habitat dried up as a result of climate change. This shows the extent of the damage caused by global warming.

◄ *In Costa Rica, the golden toad has lost its natural habitat as a result of climate change.*

## Warmer nests

Many birds seem to be benefiting from global warming. In the U.K., birds can breed further north as temperatures increase. They are also building nests earlier in the year, lengthening their breeding period. In 1998, a survey found that populations of 33 species had increased. In the cold of the Scottish highlands, local birds such as the dotterel and the ptarmigan could be in trouble as other birds move in to share their food.

Environmentalists are monitoring 281 other freshwater species, half of which are becoming rarer.

## Wildlife on the move

All over the world, as temperatures rise, wildlife is on the move. Insects are able to live in places that were previously too cold for them. In New Orleans, frost used to kill most cockroaches. Warmer, frost-free winters has resulted in a plague of cockroaches.

The mosquito is also spreading into new areas. These blood-sucking insects spread diseases such as malaria. Scientists think that two or three million more people will die from malaria in the next 100 years, as mosquitoes move into southern Europe and other parts of the world.

## In hot water

As our planet warms, so do the oceans. Areas near the poles are warming the most. Populations of salmon have declined in the North Pacific and scientists predict that they will head north to the colder waters of the Bering Sea.

Warmer seas are destroying the world's coral reefs. When the water they live in heats up, reefs become stressed and throw out the tiny plants that provide them with food. This is called coral bleaching. In 1998, the hottest sea temperatures ever were recorded. Every tropical reef in the world was affected by coral bleaching and it will take up to 100 years for them to recover. Coral bleaching could happen every year if global warming continues.

▲ The beautiful and varied wildlife of this coral reef in Papua New Guinea is, like reefs all over the world, at risk from global warming.

# Deadly chemicals

*Over the last 50 years, farmers have used more and more deadly chemicals to control unwanted weeds and insects. Most fields now have few pests and wild plants, but some chemicals have had a devastating effect on wildlife.*

## The peregrine falcon

Many of the chemical poisons used to kill weeds and insect pests were developed as war weapons. Over the last few years, they have been sprayed in ever-greater amounts onto the fruit and vegetables that we eat. Herbicides have killed native plants, while pesticides have killed insects, birds, fish, and other animals. In the U.S., the pesticide DDT killed nearly all the peregrine falcons. Numbers fell to 324, then DDT was banned in 1972

▲ A female peregrine falcon feeds its chick. The number of peregrine falcons is now rising.

and the peregrine falcons came back. In 1999, there were 1,650 in the U.S. and Canada, and the species was taken off the endangered list.

▼ Pesticides and herbicides spread by tractors and airplanes run off into nearby rivers and affect the wildlife.

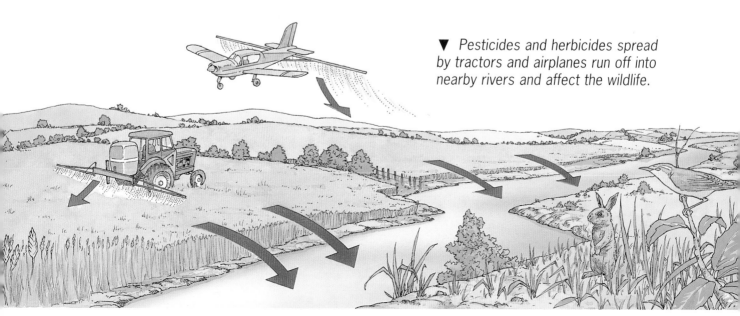

## No poisons, please

Concern about the effect of pesticides and herbicides on people has led many scientists, including the U.S. Environmental Protection Agency, to suggest that all fresh fruit and vegetables should be washed, scrubbed, and peeled before being eaten. These precautions will not be necessary if farmers use a new safe herbicide that has been developed by a German company. The herbicide contains diflufenzopyr, which kills broadleafed plants in fields, but is less poisonous to wildlife and less harmful to the environment. In 1999, the U.S. and Canada worked together to rush through approval of the new herbicide.

## Amphibians at risk

When children in Minnesota, began finding deformed frogs, scientists investigated. They found that many **amphibians**, including frogs, toads, and newts, were suddenly becoming rare. The same thing was happening all over the world. Amphibian species have become extinct in Australia, Panama, and the U.S., and everywhere else populations have declined. Scientists think that pesticides and herbicides are the main causes of this decline. These poisons are washed off the fields, and run into the streams and lakes where amphibians live.

## The dying sea

Industrial waste, sewage, and oil spills are turning the world's largest inland sea into a dead zone. Most of the pollution in the Caspian Sea comes from Russia and Azerbaijan. The amount of oil in Azerbaijan's water is 500 percent more than is allowed. Every year, Russia dumps billions of cubic yards of sewage. All this pollution spreads out to affect the whole sea, with the result that 23 wildlife species are endangered. A plan to lay an oil pipeline across the sea bed is now worrying local people. A split pipe would release so much oil into the water that wildlife would be completely devastated.

▼ Oil pollution is particularly heavy on the Azerbaijan shore of the Caspian Sea.

# Hunting and fishing

*Early humans used spears and bows and arrows to catch individual animals. Today, guns make hunting a one-sided sport and industrial ships can sweep whole areas of the sea clean of fish.*

## Bear hunting

People in British Columbia, Canada, no longer eat grizzly bears—but hunters still buy licenses to kill them. About 350 bears die each year, and at least 175 more are shot illegally. No one knows how many grizzly bears are left, but some conservationists estimate only 4,000. At this rate, the grizzly bear's days are numbered.

▲ *This shark has been killed for its fin. Shark's fin soup is an Asian favorite, the centerpiece of Chinese banquets.*

## Shark's fin soup

Sharks were swimming in the sea 400 million years ago, long before dinosaurs appeared. The adults have no natural predators, and live long lives. Unlike other fish that produce thousands of babies, most of which do not survive to adulthood, sharks have few offspring. Fishing now kills 70 million sharks each year. Many are killed illegally for their fins, to make soup. Indonesian fishermen hook sharks, hack off their fins, and leave the injured sharks to die in the sea. Boats have been found with 800 fins stored on board. Several shark species are endangered by this brutal trade.

◄ *A young, black bear has been shot by a hunter. Unlike animal predators hunting for food, humans also kill for sport.*

▲ *The environmental group Greenpeace has been active in the campaign to stop Norwegian whaling.*

## Save the whale

For a thousand years, whales have provided meat, oil for lamps, and fat for candles and soap. Blue whales are the largest animals ever to live on Earth, and there were once a quarter-of-a-million of them in the oceans. Today, only about 1,000 are left.

Unlike sharks, blue whales and other species are protected by a worldwide agreement that bans whaling. But in Japan, Korea, and Norway, whale meat is still popular. In 1993, Norwegian ships began catching whales again. Every year they catch more—671 in 1998 and 753 in 1999. Japanese ships also catch whales, but they say this is only for scientific purposes. The result is the same: fewer whales survive, and some species are endangered. Many people have protested against whaling, and organizations such as Greenpeace campaign to stop the slaughter.

## Double standards

Native Americans in Canada have been trapping mink, fox, and beaver for hundreds of years. As some land is poor, farming cannot provide all their food. Selling fur has made the difference between survival and death for many of these tribal communities. New laws have stopped the sale of fur from trapped animals, but some tribal people have little hope of other work. They suggest that modern factory farms, which rear chickens in huge sheds and pigs in tiny concrete stalls, are far more cruel than trapping, but the laws remain.

# Introduced species

*When an animal or plant is introduced to a place where it has not previously lived, it mixes with the local wildlife. Sometimes, the effects can be devastating.*

## Oceans apart

For millions of years, the wildlife in the Mediterranean Sea was quite different from that in the Red Sea. This changed when the Suez Canal was opened in 1869, allowing ships to travel between the two seas. Gradually, species from the Red Sea moved through the canal into the Mediterranean Sea. So far, about 250 different species have made the trip, competing with local species for food and driving many away. Only the fittest will survive the invasion.

The Red Sea jellyfish is a recent arrival in the Mediterranean. It was first spotted in 1977, and by 1990 a continuous line of jellyfish lay along the coast of Israel. Fishermen could no longer work, and bathers left the beaches for fear of being stung. The jellyfish will probably continue to spread along the coasts of North Africa, Greece, Italy, France, and Spain.

▼ *The Suez Canal allows both ships and marine wildlife to travel between the Mediterranean and the Red Sea.*

▲ *Cane toads gather at night under a streetlight in Australia.*

## A plague of toads

In 1935, giant marine toads from South America were introduced into fields of sugar cane in Queensland, Australia, to eat beetles that were damaging the sugar. But soon the cane toads, as Australians call them, became pests themselves.

The skin of cane toads is poisonous, so snakes and other predators avoid them. They breed in large numbers and eat other amphibians, insects, fish, birds, and small mammals. In northeastern Australia cane toads gather by the hundred in gardens and on roads. They are now more of a problem than the beetles they were brought in to eat. And they are on the move, extending their range all the time as their population grows.

When mealybugs (below) destroyed crops in St. Kitts, in the Caribbean, farmers decided against using chemical poisons. Instead, they introduced stingless wasps that normally live in China. When these wasps are released in a crop, they lay eggs in the mealybugs. The eggs hatch into maggots and kill the mealybugs. In two years, the wasps had reduced the mealybug population by 94 percent. In 1999, mealybugs were spotted in California, and officials estimated they would cause $750 million dollars worth of damage if allowed to spread. They quicklysent for the stingless wasps.

# Destroyed habitats

*Wild animals and plants die when their habitat is destroyed. As more land is cleared to build roads and towns, and to create farmland, more habitats disappear.*

## Ancient meadows

Meadows, where many species of wild flowers mix with grasses, have provided hay for farm animals for hundreds of years. The hay is cut in the fall and used during the winter. Several species of bumble bees rely on meadows for food and shelter. Modern agriculture has destroyed most meadows. Fields are cut before plants have a chance to seed and herbicides restrict the range of wild flowers that are able to survive.

In 1998, the short-haired bumble bee became extinct in Britain. Over the previous 50 years, 95 percent of ancient meadows had disappeared. Other bees are also endangered in the U.K. The shrill carder bee is found in only seven places. The rest of its habitat has changed as a result of modern farming methods.

▼ *In Europe, natural meadows are now rare. Many wild plants grow in this Spanish meadow, including poppies, daisies, and almond trees.*

## Protect and survive

About 175 million years ago, Madagascar was part of a huge continent called Pangea. When the continents of Africa and India moved away from each other, Madagascar became an island. Since then, the wildlife has evolved differently from anywhere else. Much of the unique wildlife lives in the rich forests, but more than 90 percent of these have been cut. In 1999, the Andringitra National Park was opened, protecting more than 75,000 acres of forest, grassland and mountain habitats. There are 30 orchid species in the new park, and 14 species of lemur, including the golden bamboo lemur (below), which was discovered in 1996.

## Rare rabbits

The forests on two islands in southern Japan are home to amami rabbits. This species is similar to fossils that have been found of ancient rabbits. The Japanese have protected the amami rabbit by law, calling it a national monument, but that has not stopped the species becoming endangered. Dogs and cats kill them, and some are still hunted and used in traditional medicines. In addition, over the last 20 years 95 percent of the forests where they live have been cut.

## Back from the brink

In Europe, boletus mushrooms are highly prized by cooks. On fall mornings people go into the woods to collect them. One variety, satan's boletus, is found only in oak and beech woods. Modern plantations do not support such slow-growing trees, and so the number of oak and beech trees in Europe has dropped. Satan's boletus is now so rare that special areas have been set aside where it can grow undisturbed in its natural habitat.

▲ Satan's boletus is poisonous raw, but harmless and tasty when it is cooked. Even so, most collectors avoid it.

# Wildlife in the future

*Around the world conservation groups are working to ensure that endangered animals and plants survive. In the future pressures on wildlife will increase—so it is important that we continue and extend conservation work.*

## Out of the cage

Many zoos started as museums, displaying examples of different species in cages. Today, zoos allow animals as much freedom as possible— and they play a crucial role in conservation by breeding endangered wildlife. When the last few Arabian oryx were threatened with death by poachers, some animals were caught and encouraged to breed in zoos. Eventually, the last oryx living in the wild was killed, but zoos have been able to reintroduce some of their animals into the wild.

## Vacations in the wild

Tourism is one of the world's largest industries. **Eco-tourism**, which allows tourists to see animals in the wild, is increasing in popularity. Money from tourists is paying for the survival of many species. In Africa, elephants that used to be hunted for their ivory are worth more alive and free in their

▲ *The Arabian oryx has been reintroduced into the wild, but numbers are still small.*

natural habitat. But large numbers of tourists may trample plants and make animals nervous. In Uganda, mountain gorillas face three or four groups of tourists every day, waving cameras only a few yards from them. Stressed gorillas have begun charging at the tourists. Eco-tourism will continue to grow, but it will benefit both people and wildlife only if it is properly managed.

## Watching the animals

New technology allows conservationists to track wild animals and make sure they are safe. In Kenya's Tsavo National Park and South Africa's Madikwe Reserve, rhinos have been fitted with radio-tracking collars. Wardens can follow the movements of the rhinos without disturbing them and protect them from poachers. Radio collars have also been fitted to wild dogs in South Africa's Kruger Park. These collars emit signals that are picked up by satellite. Scientists thousands of miles away in Scotland can track the dogs' movements. Similar satellite tracking is watching polar bears, turtles, and albatrosses as they travel vast distances.

▲ *These tourists have been taken by local guides to within a few yards of a mountain gorilla.*

## Inventing new species

The newly-developed technology of **genetic modification (GM)** may result in a widespread change to wildlife. In GM, scientists work with the **genes** that control every physical aspect of a plant or animal. They select a gene from one species and add it to those of another. For example, adding a fish's anti-freezing gene to a tomato has produced a frost-resistant plant. Crops can be altered so that they need less water, contain medicines, or have more vitamins. In Scotland, GM salmon grew four times quicker than normal.

No one knows what will happen when GM plants and animals mix with wildlife. Already, some species of butterfly are vanishing because the caterpillars cannot feed on the new GM crops. In the future, GM animals and plants may breed with wild species. Then wildlife will change forever.

▼ *The genetically-modified tomato on the left is much larger than the ordinary one on the right.*

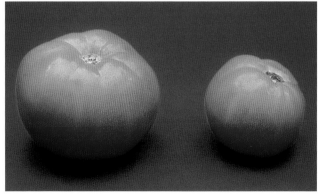

# How you can help

*The more we learn about local animals and plants, the more we appreciate the importance of wildlife everywhere.*

▲ *Nesting boxes provide a safe place for wild birds to breed and offer opportunities to observe and record bird behavior.*

## On safari

Wildlife exists on almost any land, from lonely countryside to city streets. Inner city walls harbor moss, and puddles may have a covering of slimy algae. A patch of lawn is made up of several grass species, as well as dandelions and other small flowers.

Alleys and verges are wildlife corridors, home to everything from insects to small mammals such as shrews, hedgehogs, and foxes. As you become used to looking for wildlife in all these places, you will begin to see more and more species.

Trash, such as plastic bags, can kill wild animals, so spend a few minutes clearing garbage from any wildlife habitats you explore. Never be tempted to dig up wild plants. Picking the flowers stops them attracting insects and producing seeds. If you want to record the beauty of the wildlife you find, use a camera, or make a drawing.

You need not be a great artist to make pictures of your best finds. Concentrate on just showing the overall shape and the main features. Remember to write on the place and date. If you record your finds regularly, you will soon build up a fascinating wildlife catalog.

## Beautiful butterflies

To bring wildlife to your garden, grow plants that attract butterflies. The buddleia is so attractive to butterflies that it is also called the butterfly bush. Other sweet-scented flowers such as lavender and candytuft are small enough to be grown in pots on a window-sill. Butterflies feed by drinking nectar from flowers. Their wings are delicate, so do not touch them. Other insects, such as beetles and hoverflies, will also be attracted. Identify them and make a list with the date, time of day, and the weather.

## Grow your own wildlife

If you have access to a garden, you can turn part of it into a wildlife habitat. Wild-flower seeds can be bought at garden centers. A pond is a haven for insects, water creatures, plants, birds, and frogs. It need not be large or expensive to make. Even a pond as small as 3 feet square will attract a wide variety of wildlife.

Once you have access to a wildlife habitat, watch it change with the seasons. Wildlife will develop as new plants dominate and new animals come to live there. Keep the habitat clear of trash—and encourage others to look after a small space for wildlife.

▲ *A garden pond looks attractive and will soon be full of wildlife.*

▲ *A buddleia is easy to grow and will attract many butterflies. Here two butterflies are drinking nectar from the flowers.*

## Getting involved

All over the world people get together to help save endangered wildlife. Non-governmental organizations (NGOs) work to conserve wildlife in many different ways. Some campaign against human activity that threatens the habitats of wildlife, while others concern themselves with cruelty to animals. NGOs give us all a chance to take action. They encourage us to learn more about wildlife, and will provide information. You can help by becoming a member, or by raising money to send. You will find useful addresses on pages 44–5 of this book.

# Wildlife projects

*Here are three projects that will help you observe the wildlife around you.*

## Feed the birds

In winter, birds have difficulty finding food, and a cold spell may result in many birds starving. A bird-table, stocked twice a day with food, will attract a variety of species that you will be able to watch.

The table should be raised 5 feet above the ground. Choose a position near a tree or hedge on which the birds can settle, but not so close that cats can pounce on the feeding birds. You can buy bird seed from a pet store or supermarket. Kitchen scraps and brown bread will also be welcomed. Hang a feeder for nuts from the table to attract some birds. Others do not readily visit a bird-table. Scatter seed on open ground for them.

Feed the birds once a day, in the morning, from mid-fall through to mid-spring. In really cold weather feed twice a day. But beware of feeding loose peanuts and other hard foods in spring, because these may choke nestlings.

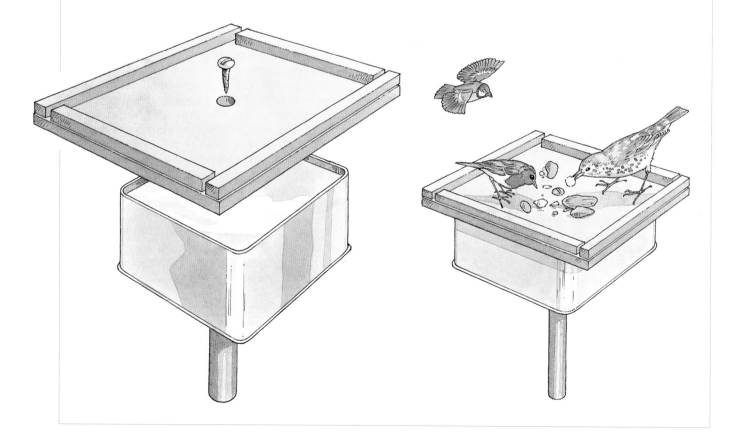

# Tiny worlds

There are more than a million different kinds of insects, more than all other animal species put together. Why not catch some insects with a net or jar, and examine them through a magnifying glass? You can find out what species they are using an insect guide.

At night, a light left outside will attract dozens of different insect species that can be caught with a net. A pitfall trap (right) will catch beetles. Sink a jar into the soil so that the opening is level with the ground. Make a roof to keep rain out by supporting a square of wood on four stones. Small pieces of cheese or meat will attract insects into the jar and they won't be able to climb back out again.

Another way to catch insects is to spread a sheet under a branch and then tap the branch so that any insects fall on to the sheet. Study the insects you find, looking at any markings, the shape of the head, and the legs. Always release the insects afterwards, taking them back to where they were caught.

You could test different areas when you visit friends or go on vacation.

## Rotten stuff

A rotting log of wood develops an eco-system of its own, which will include fungi, plants, and animals. You can study this by finding a rotten log. Alternatively, place a log or scrap of untreated wood on the ground and wait until it rots. Collect the insects and try to identify them. Count the types of vegetation living on the log. There may be lichens and moss, and possibly mushrooms and patches of fungus. When you have finished your study, find a quiet place to leave the log, so that its eco-system can continue undisturbed.

# Wildlife facts and figures

## Largest and smallest

The largest animals ever to live on the land were dinosaurs. The skeleton of one shows an animal 131 feet long. It may have weighed as much as 110 tons.

There are billions of corals in a reef. The Great Barrier Reef off the coast of Queensland, Australia, is the largest structure built by living creatures. Scientists think the coral started gathering there over 600 million years ago.

Bacteria are the smallest living things on Earth. Each bacterium consists of a single cell. Compare that with your body, which contains about a million million (1,000,000,000,000) cells.

The largest animal alive today is the blue whale. A blue whale caught in 1947 measured over 88 feet, and weighed 209 tons.

The seeds of the giant fan palm can weigh more than 45 pounds. If you put one seed on a pair of scales, you would need 200 billion (200,000,000,000) orchid seeds to balance it. Orchid seeds are the world's tiniest seeds, each one weighing only 3½ millionths of 1 ounce.

The rafflesia, which grows in the rainforests of the Amazon, produces a flower about one yard in diameter, and weighing over 24 pounds—the world's biggest flower.

The leaves of the *Victoria amazonica* water lily are so big and strong that a child could stand on one of them.

## Oldest plant

The oldest individual plant is a king's holly in Tasmania, thought to be more than 40,000 years old.

The oldest tree in the world is a redwood that has stood in Prairie Creek National Park in California for 12,000 years.

## New species

In 1997 scientists investigating a cave in Spain found 16,000 species of wildlife that had never before been recorded.

## Rarest species

The world's rarest duck species lives on an island off the coast of New Zealand. The group of 20 sub-Antarctic teal is the only group left in the wild. Ducks on the mainland were killed by rats and wild cats. In 1999, conservationists released 12 sub-Antarctic teal that had been bred at a wildlife center on the island. They were fitted with radio transmitters so their movements could be followed.

There are several species of giant tortoise, some of which are very rare. Only one Abingdon Island giant tortoise is known. It is an old male, and when he dies the species will become extinct.

The rarest animal in Asia is probably a sub-species of the Javan rhino that lives in Vietnam. Conservationists believe there are between five and eight of these one-horned rhinos left, but they have never seen one. They have only been able to study footprints and droppings. In 1999, an automatic camera took the first-ever photos of the Vietnamese Javan rhino.

# Wildlife around the world

*By looking at these maps, you can compare areas where wildlife is at risk with areas where it is protected in parks and reserves. People have never before had such power over wildlife and its future.*

Wildlife is endangered the world over. On every continent, animals and plants that have adapted to the local environment are under threat. But the threats vary. In richer countries, such as Europe and the U.S., much of the original vegetation was cleared long ago. Natural habitats disappeared at the same time. Industry and intensive farming are widespread, leading to threats from pollution. In African and South American countries, large areas of natural vegetation remain. As these are cleared habitats are lost.

## Endangered species around the world

▼ *This map shows where some of the endangered species in the book are found in the wild. All may become extinct unless we continue our efforts to save them.*

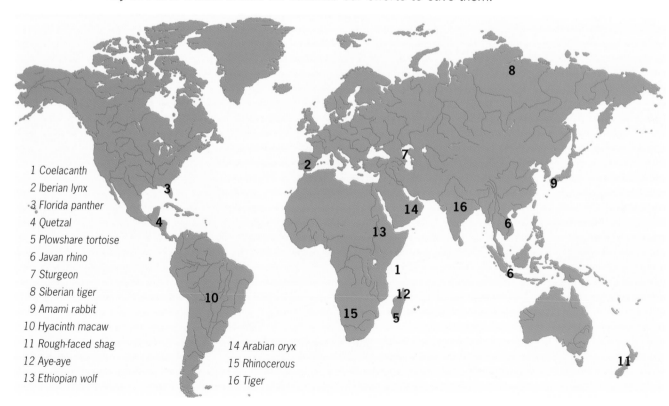

1 Coelacanth
2 Iberian lynx
3 Florida panther
4 Quetzal
5 Plowshare tortoise
6 Javan rhino
7 Sturgeon
8 Siberian tiger
9 Amami rabbit
10 Hyacinth macaw
11 Rough-faced shag
12 Aye-aye
13 Ethiopian wolf
14 Arabian oryx
15 Rhinocerous
16 Tiger

# Protected areas around the world

▼ *Most countries have areas where wildlife is protected. National parks are run by governments, with laws to stop hunting and poaching. Nature reserves are areas set aside to allow wildlife to live in peace.*

● national park

■ nature reserve

# Threats to wildlife around the world

▼ *People today have greater power over wildlife than ever, destroying and polluting habitats, killing animals with modern weapons, and introducing new species which threaten existing ones.*

■ habitat loss

▲ poaching and capture

● pollution

✳ introduced species

# Further information

*Many organizations supply information about the conservation of endangered species or cruelty to animals. You can find out more by looking at their websites, or sending a large, stamped, self-addressed envelope for their latest news.*

## WORLDWIDE CONCERN (NGOs)

**The Amazing Environmental Organizations Web Directory** Earth's biggest environmental search engine, can detail topics related to wildlife and habitats.
http://www.webdirectory.com/

**ECO News** (Environmental News Service)
P.O. Box 351419, Los Angeles,
California 90035–9119

**EnviroLink Network** is the largest online environmental information resource.
5808 Forbes Avenue, Pittsburgh, PA 15217
http://www.envirolink.org

**Friends of the Earth (FoE)** one of the largest network of environmental groups in the world. Quarterly magazine *Earth Matters* includes news of environmental campaigns
1025 Vermont Avenue, NW,
Washington D.C. 20005
http://ww.foe.org

**Greenpeace** campaigns against pollution, over-fishing, and any other human activity that threatens wildlife. They can provide leaflets, educational material, and they have a website for young people.
1436 U. Street, NW, Washington D.C. 20009
http://www.greenpeaceusa.org

**National Wildlife Federation** takes action on issues. Publications and magazines.
8925 Leesburg Pike, Vienna, Virginia 22184
http://www.nwf.org

◄ *People of all ages gather at a "Save the Whale" rally in London, England.*

**Oxfam** helps people worldwide to improve their lives and care for the environment.
26 West Street, Boston, Massachusetts 02111
http://www.oxfam.america.org/

**Rainforest Action Network**
221 Pine Street, Suite 500, San Francisco, California 94104

**Worldwide Fund for Nature (WWF)** founded in 1961, and has nearly five million supporters, with groups active in 100 countries. It is one of the few NGOs to concern itself with all wildlife, aiming to save threatened species in their habitats. WWF produces reports and lleaflets, and runs an internet site.
1250 24TH Street, NW, Washington D.C. 20037–1175
http://www.worldwildlife.org/

▼ *These children are helping to plant trees as part of a program to improve the habitat for wildlife.*

# Further reading
*From Birth to Death* by Irene Yates
(Belitha Press, 1996)
*The Hunt for Food* by Anita Ganeri
(Belitha Press, 1996)
*Rainforests* by Sara Oldfield
(Cherrytree Books, 1995)
*The Atlas of Endangered Species* by Steve Pollock (Belitha Press, 1993)
*What is A?* series
*Amphibian, Bird, Fish, Insect, Mammal,* and *Reptile* by Robert Snedden
(Belitha Press, 1994)
*Nature Watch* series
*The Living Tree, The Living Pond, The Living River,* and *The Living House* by Nigel Hester (Watts, 1991)
*Collins Pocket Guides* series
*Acting for Nature:What Young People Around the World are Doing to Protect the Environment* by Sneed et al
(Heyday Books, 2000)

**OTHER USEFUL CONTACTS**
**World Conservation Monitoring Center** runs a Threatened Plants Database. This can be accessed on its website: wcmc.org.uk

Other websites with information on wildlife:
**Bagheera**
http://www.bagheera.com/default.htm
**African Wildlife Foundation**
http://www.awf.org
**Centre for Marine Conservation**
http://www.cmc-ocean.org
**Elephanteria** http://www.wildheart.com

# Glossary

**aerobic** Organisms that need to take in oxygen directly from air or water. Most organisms are aerobic, but some bacteria are not.

**amphibians** Animals, such as newts and frogs that lay eggs in water, have young that live in water—but they develop lungs and legs that allow survival on land.

**bacteria** Tiny living things that help to break down dead plants and animals.

**bio-region** An area that has a distinct balance of living things.

**biosphere** The layer around planet Earth where life is found.

**cladistics** A modern way of grouping species by looking at the way they have evolved.

**classification** Grouping different plants and animals together by finding similarities.

**conservation** Protecting wildlife and the environment.

**cyanobacteria** A type of bacteria that can convert sunlight into food, as plants do. This is the basis of plant life on Earth today.

**DNA** The carrier of a living thing's genetic information.

**eco-system** A group of plants and animals that live and support each other in a particular place.

**eco-tourism** Tourists traveling to see wildlife in its natural habitat.

**El Niño** A warm Pacific current that reaches the west coast of South and Central America once every six to eight years, changing the weather and affecting wildlife.

**endangered species** A species of plant or animal that seems likely to become extinct.

**evolution** The natural process that takes place over millions of years, with animals and plants developing characteristics allowing them to survive better.

**extinct** A species that no longer has a living representative.

**extinction** The end of a species, when no more remain alive.

**food chain** The transfer of food and nutrients from one living thing to another.

**food web** The food chains in an eco-system.

**fossil** Part of a living thing from long ago preserved in rock.

**gene** One of the units of DNA that passes on characteristics from parents to offspring.

**genetic modification (GM)** Changing, or modifying, the genes of plants and animals (the parts that give them their individual characteristics).

**grazing animals** Animals that eat plants.

**habitat** The environment in which a plant or animal naturally lives.

**herbicides** Chemicals used to kill unwanted plants.

**hunter-gatherers** Communities that hunt animals and fish for food, and gather fruit and vegetables that grow in the wild.

**larvae** An early stage in the life cycle of invertebrates, amphibians, and fish.

**nutrients** Chemicals that provide food for a living thing.

**orthodox classification** A modern way of grouping living things that still looks for similarities.

**oxygen** A gas that makes up 21 percent of the air. It supports animal life and allows fires to burn.

**pesticides** Chemicals used by farmers to kill unwanted animals.

**phenetic classification** A way of grouping species that exist into large groups.

**poacher** Someone who breaks the law by entering someone else's land to kill an animal.

**predator** An animal that catches other animals to kill and eat them.

**prey** An animal killed and eaten by a predator.

**rare species** A type of animal or plant that exists in only a few protected areas.

**savannah** Grassland in hot dry places.

**scientific name** A name consisting of two Latin words. Every species has its own Latin name.

**species** A group of animals or plants that are alike and can breed together.

**threatened species** A species of plant or animal common in a few places, whose numbers are falling.

**trilobite** One of the earliest-known animals on Earth, identified only from fossil remains.

**wildlife** Any living thing that exists without humans looking after it.

**zoologist** A scientist who studies animals.

# Index